T0162090

UNDERGROUND RIVERS

BY PEGGY SHUMAKER

Esperanza's Hair
The Circle of Totems
Braided River (chapbook)
Wings Moist from the Other World

Peggy Shumaker

Underground Rivers

poems

RED HEN PRESS   LOS ANGELES 2002

Underground Rivers
Copyright © 2002 by Peggy Shumaker

All rights reserved.

No part of this book may be used or reproduced in any manner whatever without written permission except in the case of brief quotations embodied in critical articles and reviews.

Author photo by Barry McWayne
Cover design by Wanda Chin
Book design by Mark E. Cull

First Edition
ISBN 1-888996-50-1
Library of Congress Catalog Card Number: 2001097532

Printed in Canada

Second printing November 2003

Published by: **Red Hen Press**
            www.redhen.org

For Joe

ACKNOWLEDGMENTS

Many thanks to the editors and publishers of the journals and anthologies which published these poems, sometimes in earlier versions:

Amicus Journal: "Ajo Lily"; *Ascent*: "Rio Santa Cruz, Arroyo Santa Cruz"; *Blackbird*: "Night-Blooming Jasmine"; *Hayden's Ferry Review*: "Refuge"; *Looking North*: "Avalanche Lily," "The Story of Light," "What to Count on," "What Will Remain"; *Nimrod*: "What Will Remain," titled "Wingspan of Sand"; *Phoebe*: "Snowflake Eel"; *Prairie Schooner*: "Aubade: Morning Aurora," "Bear Plan, Brooks Range," "Grace," "Hillclimb"; *Puerto del Sol*: "Too Soon After Rain"; *Quarterly West*: "Crossing the Pacific," "Underground Rivers"; *The Salt River Review*: "Hunger on the Wing"; *Steam Ticket*: "Avalanche Lily," "Orange Peel," "Owls' Cough Balls"; *Third Coast*: "What to Count On"; *Under Northern Lights*: "Locket"; *West Branch*: "Easter, Grave Tending"; *Weber Studies*: "Pantano Wash."

Thanks to the many writer friends who gave time and care to drafts of these poems: Burns Cooper, Steve Gehrke, Cynthia Hogue, John Morgan, Paul Morris, Kathy Murphy, John Reinhard, Frank Soos, Steve Styers. Special thanks to Christianne Balk, Anne Caston, and Alberto Ríos.

Thanks to the University of Alaska Fairbanks for a sabbatical during which several of these poems were written.

Thank you to the staff and students at the Stadler Center for Poetry at Bucknell University, for a residency that gave me time to revise. Thank you to Mr. Stadler.

Thanks beyond measure to Joe Usibelli.

CONTENTS

Hunger on the Wing

The Story of Light

Camouflage

Grace

At the spring
we hear the great seas traveling
underground,
giving themselves up
with tongues of water
that sing the earth open.

—Linda Hogan, "To Light"

HUNGER ON THE WING

TOO SOON AFTER RAIN

(Sonoran desert, where the dead
are said to cherish fragrances)

Too soon after rain blue woman
takes a step toward her mother
long gone, that memory an aroma

of cilantro gathered from
tree wells. Sopa fideo, no bother
so soon after rain. The woman

wants to recall her future. Not the one
she will live, but the dreamt other
long gone, a mother's legacy. This aroma:

a sweaty man, welcome,
pours his skyful of sorrow inside her
too soon. After rain, blue woman

walks, each footprint an omen
shaped in earth, of earth, the mother
not gone. Long memory, that aroma

of death sprouting. Dark humus
feeding us, feeding on us and all others.
Too soon. After rain blue woman's
long gone, like memory. Now, the aroma.

NIGHT-BLOOMING JASMINE

No, even though
his touch unfurls

the frowsy camellia's lack of restraint,
soothes the cool profusion of

slick-leafed calla lilies,
thumbs the tangled

tumble of honeysuckle, even so
I do not

love the man
beside me tonight.

The candles I know
by name,

the sesame oil's
skin-warmed aroma,

that second-hand moon.
Light sloshes bare skin.

Awkward thigh-step till toes touch
wood in the Japanese tub,

I try to set anchor,
ghost ship off shore.

Wild raccoons venture
out of the canyon, rest

an hour under the evening star
perched on the fence post—

inland lighthouse guiding
wayward birds of paradise.

There is no love
in the world

absent
from this moment.

This moment that slips
incognito into

small waves
breaking away

from our bodies, waves
spilling starlight

over the tub's rim,
starlight we step in,

our reflections
break, waver.

UNDERGROUND RIVERS

1.

Hillary can't cut
through the arroyo

lugging her battered
violin home. Strange

men drag couch cushions
down there, crack open

beers in their trash beds.
Arroyo men yell

at kids, each other,
holler, *hey, hey you.*

So Hillary takes
the long way around.

2.

Young ones have played here
for nine hundred years,

lifted scorpions
on ironwood sticks,

dug clay after rain,
sifted the silty

ditch sand for rubies.
Iron filings smudge

the river bottom,
twine like garter snakes

around skinny wrists.
Young ones scuff hardpan,

drag heels to mark walls—
make up houses where

they breathe the most death-
less breaths of their lives.

3.

Young ones keep secrets
rose quartz and turquoise

buried. The buzzing
saguaro, honey-

combed, throws javelins.
Lightning dry rootfans

decay in moonlight,
where two dirt-shaped men

doze, fitful, sweaty,
beside rank runoff,

stinkwater treated
better than they are

but still contagious.
One dreams of the place

when he was a boy
the Santa Cruz ran

clear before it dis-
appeared underground,

dreams of the Wishing
Shrine where he prayed hard

and lit red candles
for his father to

stay always away
so the boy wouldn't

have to kill him. Parched,
the man wakes up stiff,

jerky, his own salt
making the desert

thirstier. He has
no idea how

he will get this grit
out of his eyes, how

he will scrounge up words
to make one more day,

his dry tongue splintered
insatiable, dust,

dry tongue put to bed
with no promises.

PANTANO WASH

We rode hard
our swaybacked
dreams, loosened pebbles
with hoofpicks,
sang the stickers
out of our palms, soles,
sang the bruised foot
out from between boulders,
our family heaped
like stones on our chests.

We gave to the first one
who asked
our breath—
the hiss
of yucca
pushing out
leafshoots,
steamed oceanbeds of marrow,

the stars unfurled like fiddleheads,
our laughter the fine grain
of ironwood, streambed, eyelid,
songs our childhood
forbade us to sing
till now, till now

our tongues clacking
like palo verde beans
dropping between
dry fish hooks
splayed over the barrel's
firm skin, prickly
pear nipped
by the jazz-drunk javelina
we followed,
loping bareback,

till we could hunker down
in all our shady places,
tasting the moisture
two small stones under the tongue
returned to us.

SADDLED

Like us, Jeri Lou was too little to know
why the Kotex saddle tied to her stick horse
might cause trouble.

She galloped through unstained
meadows far greener than anything
she'd ever seen,

steeplechased sprinkler heads,
leapt free of leg braces
fitted by charity

doctors in fezzes, leapt
into pure sun, her world
beyond body, floor-length

gown of silver light,
oleander slippers, satin reins
loose in her hand...

A different kind of mother
might have laughed,
might have asked,

"Where's the saddlehorn?"
and Jeri Lou could have
said, "This one's English, mum,"

but no. Nostrils streaming Camel smoke,
Mrs. Watson yanked her in,
yelled at the rest of us *Go home*.

High in the fruitless mulberry, we
saw Jeri Lou burdened with blood.
Hers, ours, all miscarried.

When she came out,
her stick horse bareback,
tossed over one shoulder

as if she were a hobo
about to hop a freight,
she brought us a story

of fists inside us
where babies grow,
fists squeezing blood

from the moon.
We were pretty sure
Jeri Lou made it all up,

on account of her mom
never told
a story that good.

REFUGE

When they do not wish to be seen,
herons, great blue, turn themselves into
top branches of huge eucalyptus.

When she needs not to be recognized,
the fence lizard stops breathing
among monkeyflowers' woody stems.

Snowy egrets, when they wish,
turn yellow toes to worms, wiggle
till fish come, inspect their last moments as fish.

The killdeer's complaint, long-legged,
strides over marsh and trail,
traveler bearing news that gets to us.

Because they are so much themselves,
lotus take a breather, draw air
deep to keep themselves buoyant,

draw air clear down to the roots.
The acorn woodpecker puts aside
what the live oak drops.

Even as plumes of brewer saltbush
brush the underside of brown-eyed susans,
the marsh breathes change, change.

When enough rushes crowd in,
when cattails and marsh grass thicken,
when water gives way to root and leaf,

marsh to meadow,
shallow minty roots of sage
will take hold, grow in dust,

draw finches and Anna's hummers,
grow fine-haired leaves that,
luminous, deflect summer.

OWLS' COUGH BALLS

Snake season—we bushwhack
sneezing past bobbling quail

start the unoiled windmill whir of
inca doves

feigning wounds to draw us past
chicks and nest.

Globemallow, pink-eye bush,
childhood legends, lesions,

fears grown up with us—don't touch—stay
other, safe, apart. Mummy Mountain,

steep hillside named for the wrapped
and embalmed, the body hot

in its sarcophagus, graven
images outside of the idealized

ruler, divine, not guessing.
The soul sure for once—

this earth dances, palo verde
delirious yellow dances

blue-banded lizards skitter, waxy purple
petals on the prickly pear

samba their brief lives in splendor
then make way for ripe fruit.

Ocotillo for its cool day tangos
lush, abundant

stiff leaves secure
among thorns,

graceful droop of the sexual
blossoms, flamboyant

for their moment, this morning.
Foxtails' fine plum brushes

stroke, poke through to bare skin
skin still harboring

early morning chill of the snake nest,
coyote den, the burrows

of ground squirrels, the refuge
all creatures born of this earth

return to. Abandoned
radio spires

pick up signals
beyond our ken. Wiry

perches for three harbingers
among the spatters—Screech owls

cough up
what they can't digest—

minute molars, half a skull,
femur and pelvis

mashed together, mangled,
matted among clumps

of the rodents' coats
of many colors

dried fur binding
this new body, matter

immobile but filled
with stories,

lush,
left over.

RIO SANTA CRUZ,
ARROYO SANTA CRUZ

The river takes the shape of the bank it carves,
carts off yucca, pronuba, unfettered flotsam.
The arroyo by collapsing grows wide and large,

falls into itself. Dust scarves
billow, dry footholds for bur sage, hollows for snake dens.
The river takes the shape of the bank. It carves

wet clay. This potter slips past, charges
and whirls, seeks the soul undammed.
The arroyo by collapsing grows. Wide and large

the desert stretches. Shape-shifting coyotes scrounge,
unearth a nest of kangaroo rats.
The river takes the shape of the bank it carves,

leaves behind what it cannot carry.
Silt and jetsam sink, settle, calm.
The arroyo by collapsing grows wide and large

as dreams still possible, desires unspoken. Margins
of what might have been, could be, re-form.
The river takes the shape of the bank it carves.
The arroyo, by collapsing, grows wide and large.

AJO LILY

Two feet deep
under quartz and silica

under earth no path
marks off

the bulbs swell,
sweetness too deep

to lure larvae,
ground too hard

even wet years
to tempt claws.

Impossibly delicate
one layered shoot reaches up

pushing aside
massive rubble

rearranging the mosaic
of surface pebbles

so these clear blue bells
might echo

ajo, ajo
the sky's voice

moments before
first drops bruise

dry earth,
before first drops

bead jojoba pods
where the swallowtail

drinks, moments before
a new shoot

slips slick as garlic
into a world deep blue

slit by sheet lightning,
pounded by hard water

insistent that we give
what we have

only ourselves
to feed all the world's hungry.

HUNGER ON THE WING

Past the gopher hole
sunk deep as a well digger's

test bit, gopher hole clawed
right through asphalt

past the jovial mutt's
loose dirt shimmy

under chain link,
past the frenetic stashes

of stacked-up mail,
we walk into the redtails'

open season, hawk/
grace/hunger

on the wing.
When talons snatch

her up, the blue
lizard flies.

THE STORY OF LIGHT

Estoy, mirando, oyendo,
con la mitad del alma en el mar y la mitad del alma en la tierra
y con los dos mitades del alma
miro el mundo.

—Pablo Neruda,
   "Sexual Water"

I am here, watching, listening,
with half of my soul at sea and half of my soul on land,
and with both halves of my soul
I watch the world.

—tr. by James Wright and Robert Bly

TWO THOUSAND CRANES

Two thousand cranes, not origami

Two thousand cranes grazing barley

Two thousand cranes
      panicked by eagles, buzzed
      by too-near hot-air balloons

Two thousand cranes
      meandering Creamer's marshy pasture,

      red eyebands
      slashing gray sky

Two thousand cranes, gone
      gone as summer

THE STORY OF LIGHT

Think of the woman who first touched fire
to a hollow stone filled with seal oil,
how she fiddled with fuel and flame
until blue shadows before and after her
filled her house, crowded
the underground, then
fled like sky-captains
chasing the aurora's whale tail
green beyond the earth's curve.
Her tenth summer, the elders let her
raise her issum, seal pup orphaned
when hunters brought in her mother,
their grins of plenty
broad, red. The women
slit the hard belly.
Plopped among the ruby innards
steaming on rough-cut planks
blinked a new sea-child
whose first sound
came out a question
in the old language, a question
that in one throaty bark
asked *who*, meaning What family
is this? What comfort
do you provide for guests?
Do you let strangers remain
strangers? The women rinsed the slick pup
in cool water, crafted a pouch
for her to suck. Then the young girl
whose hands held light
even when the room did not
brought this new being
beside her bed, let it scatter

babiche and split birch
gathered for snowshoes, let it
nose the caribou neck hairs
bearding her dance fans. They
held up the fans to their foreheads,
playing white hair, playing old.
In the time when women do not sew
the seal danced at her first potlatch.
And when the lamps burned down,
no one could see
any difference between waves
in rock, waves in sea.
The pup lifted her nose, licked
salt from seven stars, and slipped
light back among silvers and chum
light among the ghostly belugas
swimming far north to offer themselves.

HAUL ROAD

Twenty years ago,
primacord and front end loaders
uprooted this whole

watershed, loosened
dirt tied up
in root wads, blew

the ground's cover.
The dragline
scraped away

overburden
concealing coal
soon to be burnt

into electricity.
After trucking out
forty foot seams, twenty foot

seams, gleaned
skinny seams,
the miners

re-sculpted the hills,
broadcast
mixed seed from the air,

gave dust
dusty yellow
canola to hang onto until

willow and cranberry
reinvaded. Grown taller
than our pickup, good browse,

willow covers our tracks.
Hidden, your hard miner's palm
lifts from coal-colored lace

the sunwarmed hillside
of my breast, your mouth
seismic, turbulent

as we reclaim
one small patch,
August afternoon.

BEAR PLAN, BROOKS RANGE

Groggy in the half-life
just before sleep

snug up against you, limbs
pruned by the narrow bunk,

I jostle this first night
rowdy in the sleeping cabin

gnawed by porcupines. I murmur
over the murmur of a new hatch—

mosquitoes flocking black net
nailed neatly about our bunk,

murmur one question
asking not so much for an answer

but reassurance beyond your calm
drowsy scent naked and safe.

What's our bear plan?
Han bolts awake—*Bear plan?*

We have a bear plan? This afternoon
after bumping over the dotted line

at the Arctic Circle, after
yelling out at first sight,

jubilant, *There she is,*
The Mighty Yukon, after

landing the Widgeon
belly first, skimming the undisturbed

surface of Walker Lake,
propwash skittering

frantic pellets over plexiglass,
we yawned to clear

full ears, pulled on
hipwaders, ferried our few days'

supplies to shore. Something big
had been here,

big enough, say,
to rip away both boat shed

doors, to leave hinges
bent into question marks

or snapped, metal
jagged as the Arrigetch, peaks

broken, heaved, slammed
into being.

Hanna found the footprints,
pigeontoed, along the shore,

claw to heel half again longer
than her oversized sneakers,

wider than her amazed face.
We cache our food far

from where we'll sleep, cook
and wash up away

from where we'll spread
our bedrolls. What's

our bear plan? Joe, the one
among us born and raised here, says,

Make a lot of noise.
First time here, Han says,

That's it? Then Joe admits
he's brought a gun.

In the plane. And we picture it, fifty yards
down the beach,

across the bear path,
floating in thigh-high

ice water, picture too
our diaper waddle

swaddled in waders, and know
just how tenuous is

our brief time here.
One by one we drop off,

exhausted by possibilities,
wake to cub tracks

criss-crossing the tabula rasa
at the water's edge,

marvel at billows
of white butterflies

feeding on delicacies
we can't even see,

hollow black earth
turned in the night

by great curved claws
of ones watching

who do not allow themselves
to be seen.

ORANGE PEEL

Inside the Monsoon
       out of sight of perfect stars
              crossed and the cleft moon

a man and a woman kill time
       before the late show.
              Herbal tea, one orange.

The peel slips free effortlessly, his
       bitten nails stinging,
              the light citrus sheen.

One section on his tongue,
       he thinks to offer her one,
              but finds his thought

interrupted. Her thousand questions, pokes
       in the ribs, nudges,
              hints how her lip

the one she's chewing now
       might linger on his . . .
              —No. He has decided.

Practices telling her
       "My eye is on
              another target."

She has never thought of a woman
       as a target.
              When she asks, "What

are you afraid of?"
        he attacks. She watches
            the backs of his hands.

He arranges the broken orange peel
        so it tells for him the story
            of his people forced

to leave along the road frozen solid.
        First the samovar, then the menorah,
            then the clumsy bundles

of their dead
        they left
            frozen solid beside the rut

out of that country, across oceans
        into a life where people
            tear their clothes

on purpose, so others will want to touch
        them, and she does, she touches
            his downy knee

through the grin of denim.
        He wills this to mean
            nothing, as he does

the way she takes his hand
        (too much too soon too bad) . . .
            She slides one male peel

into the female hollow of another.
       Cringes. They laugh.
             She is used to being the one

who must find some firm and gentle
       gesture to ease herself
             away.

The orange peel, shards
       turned up, cup
             ancient ancestral shynesses.

Under her hands, the peels' pattern
       dances—one world-sized vessel,
             one life, three strands (at least!)

reaching out—then the turning
       inside and out,
             the going, the coming

the aurora, the lifeline
       the flowering from within
             the "In the meantime, what?"

RIME

Overnight, each twig has grown
white fur, the air so still
snow throws
into sharp relief each
branch plus
each branch's crooked
light-bent sense
of self, crystallized.
Last night, your voice
roused my limbs,
warm under flannel,
licked each branch,
split, & hollow,
licked into flame the untamed
liquids, flammable, spilled
down your chin,
moisture from the heart-
wood, risen unseasonably,
springing free not just from me,
nor your snow-cloud
juices just from you,
no—these waters
rise from hot springs
at the center of the sacred,
from the little stone
overlooked, often,
plain little stone
where vibrations from each life
ever lived, each life
yet to be, gather.

BAKU, WHO FEEDS ON BAD DREAMS

More than a thousand years ago
a Japanese carver coaxed from cypress
this small toggle, netsuke, to string along
whatever a person might carry under an obi.

Part pachyderm, part lion,
with a great knobby spine
roaring through skin—Baku,
who feeds on bad dreams.

Voracious hunter, night stalker,
God who takes in
what we can't admit,
protector, devourer, in one.

Spirited backbone,
each burl an oracle bone,
(look for the lamp in that spine!)
each knot shaped by that back's burdens,

every vertebra a rung
on the ladder to the dreamtime
when soul, mind and body
blend into a single breath, eternal.

Which infernal delicacy would it savor first,
this Baku—the sweat soaked chill
of a child come to harm?
—gnarled hands with no bodies, reaching,

grabbing, holding fast? —over there,
uncovered, your most secret
secret spread on a silver platter
garnished with blood oranges, lies, regrets?

Between courses Baku tongues
your fear of death,
sorbet to clear the palate.
Entree, the meat of

all you'll never know—
the haunting why of loss
a subtle lingering sauce.
Dessert, this tart nightmare—

single section of a ripe tangerine
slipped from its skin
separated from all close company
alone alone alone. Baku chews.

AUBADE: MORNING AURORA

Dawn aurora churning
    this morning
whole sky
    a bright ether dream
the pink-tinged green
    just before consciousness
fades . . .

This morning
    your surgeon
holds in her capable hands
    the tough purple fist
of your womb, the two nubbly
    walnuts on their stalks,
ashes, ashes . . .

When you wake,
    parched,
no water allowed,
    lick your lips,
sigh through them
    a single breath
the one the lights can hear, the one
    that brings the sky
within reach

So many legends
        about the lights—
that just the right
        whistle might lure
them down, that
        wherever they touch
ground, blood
        must follow . . .

Then breathe
        cannibal dance,
red cedar, crooked
        beak of heaven.

Picture your healed self
        astride Orion
blizzard stallion
        shying from ash in wind
shying from bare-limbed birch.

CAMOUFLAGE

My bones drank water, water fell
through all my doors.

—Maxine Kumin,
"Morning Swim"

DIVE

Above, a quilt of molten glass,
the surface of time
liquid, each breath
suspended, rising
in capsules, CO_2
gleaned from our blood

Below, desire to know
how soft corals open themselves
to night, how parrotfish
sleep in slick cocoons
how shapeshifters escape,
eight arms through any exit
impossibly tiny, jagged, close

Below human need, invisible
trails of sound echo
whale to whale,
echo through oceans of time.

Below the surface,
barnacled keels, dwarf
volcanoes sharp as lava
below the cinched zodiac,
the archer, the target,
the zen letting go
below arrows of barracuda
whole quivers
shot

Below hard surge
bashing lava loose
below violet damselfish,
below gold lace
nudibranchs coupling
below the betrayal of sabertooth
blennies posing
as cleaner wrasse, then
biting

Below wrecks of commerce
or war, wrecks of pleasure
sunk into sand
below artificial reefs
laid in brine, heated
by lava flows, hatched in air—

the internal weather
of ocean inside us.

SNOWFLAKE EEL

Night dive, Okoe Bay

The snowflake eel clamps
razor teeth deep in the tail
of the mahi mahi
carcass fast turning

pure bone. Beneath
the ledge, braided in
& overslung, two
white-mouth morays, two

yellow-head morays, one
zebra eel yawn
in warning. They've drawn
the discarded skeleton

(long as a human)
close in, stripped clean
what the fisherman's quick
filet knife left behind.

The snowflake, discontented
with picked-over ribs,
levitates, mouth tight
in the tail, exposes

a cubit of wrist-thick
self. With a pit bull's frenzy,
the eel shakes the bones
so hard the luckless spine

lashes like a knotted whip.
The yellow margin on top
can't sneak his tail in edgewise,
free swims just enough to nudge

the bones back under lava.
Larger & stronger,
the big morays cast the snowflake
a look,

then gnaw the few
trailing shreds
washed in
on the light surge of evening.

CAMOUFLAGE

Night dive, Kona

We've been told
not to kneel
even if the sandy
paths between

outcrops of lava
look inviting.
That's where
crocodile eels

disappear.
And anything
that will let you
touch it,

don't. This I remember
unsteady in deep water
reaching to brace
one hand

& several tons of gear—
then I see, quick
& terrifying as any epiphany—
the rock's eyes

steady on me.
Titan scorpionfish.
This ambush
hunter, original

still life, suspends
time. My eyes trace
the great square jaw,
each stripe of fin, the toxic

spines flattened
to blend with red algae.
Vital disguise, his life
depends upon being mistaken

for stone. And mine,
at this moment upon being
not more than one breath
from my buddy,

shaking his dive light,
trying to catch my eye.
Who are we down here,
out of reach

of usual language?
Translating every gesture
of beings better adapted
to be here,

we suck our finite air
some of us calm as parrotfish
wrapped for the night in
self-made cocoons

some of us skittish
as red-speckled
octopi, remaking our shapes
each moment, each breath.

GREEN SEA TURTLES

Christmas Morning, off Kona

By the pinnacles,
effortless oval shadows
skim over us, ease
into place at the cleaning

station, where yellow
tangs and saddle wrasse
feast on sea lice,
scour algae

out of grout lines
between the turtles' tiles.
Vigilant eyes
close. A tangle of black

durgeon triggerfish
whirls, dust devil of fish.
Parrotfishes' sharp beaks
chip coral into their mouths.

What their bodies can't use
builds the beach.
I picture the beach, far off,
where the turtle we're watching

will scoop her nest,
push from her body
great masses
of unbrittle eggs.

Those long-clawed fins
will cover over the cache,
and she'll return,
an upturned cradle

rocking in surge,
to arch her pebbled neck
so lithe blue and gold
wrasse can nibble

beneath her shell's
collar. Breath heavy
as turtle shells
strapped to our back,

we immerse ourselves
one brief hour
in the larger world
we seldom see.

Whale calls
miles out
bound in.
As if on cue,

the fish as one
swarm a new arrival.
The abandoned turtle
looks both ways,

crosses the path
of our bubbles, biting
in case
some might be jellyfish,

then rises
to sun herself
as long as she likes
at the surface.

EACH RISE, EACH HOLLOW

You have taken me to a place
      where ripe papaya let go their stems
           and fell, heavy with juice, in our hands

You have taken me
      fifty feet under, swimming
          with eagle rays, while
              humpbacks above us
                  sang their way south

You have shown me the ancient madrona
      healed over barbed wire
          nailed decades ago to red bark

You have held me shivering
      before a flaring
          crosshatch of split oak

In a small plane you have lifted me
      over the San Juans,
          all of us citizens of the clouds

You have taken me to a house
      with windows to the sky,
          walls open to night

You have made me your home

You have taken me to the place
      mist barely conceals the next island,
          where each rise, veiled, each hollow
          opens, sacred

CROSSING THE PACIFIC

1.

Because even the seas get confused
sometimes, churning, rising up
to face no visible provocation,
our boat ducks back under
the Golden Gate
to wait for the ocean to earn
her name.

2.

Gay/Bi/Lesbian Pride brings to the streets
two days of unrelenting Techno—
Godzilla piledrivers
pulverizing the Embarcadero's air.
Some guy's chaps
leave cheeks bare—
fetching, no doubt, but
how can he sit? What part of need
feeds this opportunity
for chivalry?

Dykes on Bikes power-rev
past protesters who close their eyes
to secrets spelled out
in massive tattoos.
The young Asian man behind them
rollerblades alone, scanning
the crowd. He's barely
adorned, electric blue
fur diaper, glitter, and
gossamer wings not quite dry,
too delicate for the flight
he desires.

3.

We escape to quieter spectacles—
asparagus with shaved artichokes,
truffle vinaigrette, seared ahi
with wasabi-whipped mashed potatoes.
Maybe city folk rarify their meals
because too much else around
comes off as overdone . . . (As if
in Alaska my first taste of game
were not Moose Bourguignonne . . .)

4.

Our whole crew's itching to sail
beyond sight of land,
to try our unproven craft
so far out
on open ocean the horizon's
yin/yang
water/sky
is all we'll have to keep our balance.
Our shadow, foreign,
will jolt flying fish
out of salt, into air,
onto the bow. Next morning
we'll toss them, fallen stars,
back to sea.

5.

But for now, stuck, we
settle instead for the lake
under the opera house
where the half-masked god of music
steers his gondola through the gloaming.
The stand-in phantom's not scary,
but Christina, Jesus!
First she's seduced by
her own pure voice, then by the power
of submission—but wait—
she dives in past her point of no return
and spurns becoming both martyr
and messiah. By her own hand,
she recasts her course
through uncharted waters,
emerges mortal and female,
self-possessed, capable of loving.

6.

Next morning we bike to the base
of the celebrated bridge where crazed
surfers wipe out on black rocks.
Wind plays xylophone
through the small craft marina,
rigging tinging untuned masts.

Under this city forty ships
lie buried, old floating warehouses
left to silt in back when
crimps made good money
shanghaiing drunks
and rowing them out
to the merchant ships' moorings.
Today Hong Kong returns to China.
What will happen
to the women without voice
in the appointed assembly?
What will happen to the men?

7.

Along the fishing pier
Vietnamese of all ages
pull food from the sea.
The little boy hoisting a crab pot
yells for his sister to help.
Bare hooks for herring—
the smallest girl feeds hers flipping
through the narrow neck
of a two-liter pop bottle
half-filled with living silver.

The gutted skate's
fluted edges
catch sunset, just before
the Bay Bridge turns
burnished pewter.

A man who has all day
pushed his worldly goods before him
spreads a blue tarp on a bench,
his roof for the hours
till he's rousted.

Beside him, a kite
tied to the guardrail
claims its little patch of sky,
flies itself
into night.

8.

We turn ourselves over
first to sleep, then to the sea.
Beyond channel markers
a mother whale and her calf
choose us as brief companions.
The baby rolls, slapping
his huge black glistening
fin over and over.
Again. Why, we cannot know.

GRACE

You will never be alone, you hear so deep
a sound when autumn comes.

—William Stafford,
"Assurance"

AVALANCHE LILY

(the shape left after an avalanche)

Any disturbance, particle
or wave, footfall or

word, can loosen the cornice,
grease the slide,

and before a hiker
can gasp a breath,

snow spume
thunderheads

scour down
mountainsides

leaving behind
sharp-rimmed

space
no one ever saw,

though it was there, filled
with all it held

here, where restless
earth releases

at once all urges held back,
magnified, till

pure force carves
a new face

earth's transformation mask
splitting

Kwakiutl eagle's beak
yawning around salmon,

salmon mouth hooked
open around humans,

masked and slippery
unstable lily

cradle of absence
rocked by loss.

WHAT TO COUNT ON

Not one star, not even the half moon
        on the night you were born
Not the flash of salmon
        nor ridges on blue snow
Not the flicker of raven's
        never-still eye
Not breath frozen in fine hairs
        beading the bull moose's nostril
Not one hand under flannel
        warming before reaching
Not burbot at home under Tanana ice
        not burbot pulled up into failing light
Not the knife blade honed, not the leather sheath
Not raw bawling in the dog yard
        when the musher barks *gee*
Not the gnawed ends of wrist-thick sticks
        mounded over beaver dens
Not solar flares scouring the earth over China
Not rime crystals bearding a sleek cheek of snow
Not six minutes more of darkness each day
Not air water food words touch
Not art
Not anything we expect
Not anything we expect to keep
Not anything we expect to keep us alive

Not the center of the sea
Not the birthplace of the waves
Not the compass too close to true north to guide us

Then with no warning
        flukes of three orcas
                rise, arc clear of sea water

WHAT WILL REMAIN

Lit from inside, birches
spark, flare,

blaze trails
for travelers

outstretched in air.
Tawny cranes

return to rest
where earth cradles water.

Cranes graze, pace, graze, then
flap scuttle jabber scold . . .

This harvest
flashes—wingspan of sand,

hillside of crook-necks
soon to move on.

What will remain
has always remained—

water seized
by ice-driven air,

faith through hard cold
that the languages

of marsh, sky,
sandhill crane

will keep on
with us or without.

GRACE

When light stretches
from what we call
yesterday to what we call
tomorrow, the smallest
winged ones who winter over
tuck seeds in the peeled-back
scrolls of paper birch,
sunflower and millet they'll revisit
in the last gasp of light
iced over at forty below,

black capped and boreal
whisks skimming
spruce needles, skimming
last birch buds—
stylized grace
no gesture wasted,
women bending in kimono—
ancient refinement—survival's
ceremony green, startling,
frothy tea.

HILLCLIMB

I can't remember anymore
my mother's laugh, can't
recall the exact sound,
only that
it was loud and harsh and lasted
forever, har-harring its crude
way across Johnny's
so everybody stopped
chewing, and with fries
poised one end coated
red, turned to look.

No container for that laugh,
no handkerchief, no
hand-thrown mug, no
galvanized bucket, no
rough-lumber shed, no
oleander churchyard, no
glass-stained sanctuary. No
shallow grave, no
arroyo, no secret ravine. No
bowl of mountains, no
wall to wall carpet, no
greasewood, ironwood,
palo verde, mesquite.

That laugh broke the sky,
blue white shatter light
burnt crack of one world lost
piercing laser of new worlds laid open
thunder cloud-heart backlit
dusty earth-heart wide open and bare,
that laugh with a touch of molasses,

touch of delight once innocent
red-brown rainwater gushing in gutterstreams
over ankles of little kids making up
songs in their own languages,
once clear as rain-drenched
air after heat so tight
the inner membranes of nose and throat
thinned to parchment, blood hieroglyphs
dancing, shadow puppets
jerked around behind the scrim.

Then the rush—
menses, nosebleed,
iron-salt taste of blood,
our own blood, hers
so close to the surface
the simple kind gesture
of stopping her
from stepping in the path
of a speeding Duster
left five deep blue prints.
And the unkind gestures
lingered, spread purple, yellow,
crushed side of windfall lemon
no one could salvage.

That blood, that frail surface
passed down till one day
in the desert against the backdrop
of screaming Greeves and Ducati, my
unfaithful father and his delinquent
buddies ripped up fragile slopes
steep enough to flip cycles backwards.

I rooted for the hills,
not the hillclimbers. As my father
revved and revved, flailed against
and fell back from the lip
of the summit, my blood could not stay
inside one more moment. Down
my shirtfront, between my legs,
head back, down my throat,
ice held to the bridge of my nose, her
voice annoyed, saying
we should cauterize
and my visions of the tool, what tool?
what tool to burn on purpose
delicate places we want to be tougher
and how could it help
hellfire aimed toward the brain
help to cool blood flooding
the lusty slapstick of blood
undammed and breathless
the throat exposed,
hard swallows, the high drama
of dailiness, the great gulps
of blood laughs
that hurt to hear, to see.

Nobody could survive such laughter.
She didn't. Neither did I. We both
died, one to the other, as she drifted
far beyond where any hand could reach her
and I grew into the woman
her bruises, her laughter
guaranteed I'd be.

LOCKET

ONE OF THE FEW objects handed down to me when my mother died is a small rectangular locket engraved with a spray of wildflowers. Might be gold, might be plate, I don't care. It was hers. In her high school graduation portrait it rests in the hollow between her new breasts, nestled in folds of angora. Inside, a miniature photo of her, very young, her smile wide as the Milky Way. On the other side, all sleek muscles and slicked back Wildroot hair, grins a boy, a young man barely, cocky and sure he's good looking so why not cut his eyes at the camera, why not lean back on two legs of his chair, the sun's out, he's got gas money and a pretty girl, surf's up man.

During the long fifteen years of their marriage, my parents yelled at each other, didn't even agree on a topic, just yelled in general. I took solace in the knowledge of that young man, imagined he was my real dad, lost to war or adventure, his presence there next to her heart a repudiation, male and sexy, of every reproach my father could throw at her. The self she carried in that locket grinned, eternally joyous, sassy as a skirt of giant kelp, stinging bare midriff and thighs, salty as her first good kiss, not shared with my father. Nobody recalls that boy's name now, not my grandmother, not my mother's high school friends, not Uncle Harry.

And my father, what did he carry, man with no amulet to protect him, and the heavy freight of his Nazarene father always on his shoulders. Pressed down on his knees in surrender to a God he never really met, my father shook off his father's zealous palm and knelt between the knees of any willing female. "Never pass up a chance at pussy," he told Harry, who knew even at thirteen there was something basic wrong with that advice. He wasn't sure what though because all the other guys were laughing and nodding, blowing smoke rings and French inhaling. He was the youngest one there, and counted himself lucky to be allowed to tag along. So Harry swallowed hard, he told me, swallowed the hard knot in his throat and made himself think about motorcycles, baseball, ham, pistachios, anything but how his sister's, my mother's, face would look when she found out who she'd married.

CHURNING

Long before she stood at the counter
of the cream station in a rubber apron,
skimmed up a sample for the centrifuge,
whirled it, and slipped in two drops of ruby oil,
set the points of calipers
just so, careful as a snake
balancing an egg on its fangs,
delicate, the farmer watching
not that he didn't trust E.J.'s daughter
you understand but business
is business and butterfat
determines how many sacks
of flour and meal
go home in that wagon &
whether or not
a few yards will unwind
from the bolt of muslin, new
cloth for Easter, fresh skirt
for his wife's made-over
go-to-meeting dress
and the good part of the old skirt
whipped up into a waistcoat
for the baby, before that,
before prices she quoted
let Harriet know
whose skinny cow
wouldn't make it through
another Dakota winter, and whose
skinny kids wouldn't have a baked potato
to bring to school, before all that
she had one big chore—
butter.

After her father milked, & set
tall cans in the pantry,
it was her job
to scoop off
risen cream with a slotted spoon,
slip it into a half gallon
mason jar, and shake.
Forever. Shake steady,
shake long, shake
till her arms
fell off.
First she'd slosh
white water,
rapids foaming,
then watch storm clouds
thundering, then witness
the miraculous conception—
gold, arising
via her muscles, her
shaking, her will—
flecks to clumps to a solid chunk
new body luscious,
prepared to anoint
hot bread, huge farm bowls
of mashed potatoes,
legions of string beans.
Whatever the seven sisters,
their parents, and the hired hands
couldn't eat, she got to sell.
What did she save her pennies for?
Crank and a paddle—
            a mail-order churn.

MILK

Spoiled, his sisters whispered, spoiled
town girl who never learned
to milk, who snuggled down

under covers while John lit
the kitchen stove, then laced up
work boots and tramped to the barn.

Calm Norvella never needed
halter or stanchion. Eyes
closed, she sighed, relieved,

his chapped hands stripping
two strands at a time,
galvanized zings foaming.

And Harriet, new farm wife
stretching in bed,
massaged bag balm

into the just-seen planet
orbiting the milky way
of her gown, homemade

secret they could
keep only a little
while longer.

EASTER, GRAVE TENDING

Village of Moen, Norway

Just after milking, Hannah Loften
tied back her skirts and knelt
among the lettered stones,

seven generations in need
of her thick wrist twisting
nettles, scraping back

winter's scrim, her stiff bristles
scouring themselves to nubs
against chiseled names

shed by those held close in stories,
shed too by those forgotten.
Hannah Loften rinsed and weeded

till one clear star rose,
the churchyard's constellations
spiraling around her,

fading as dawn
lifted night from her eyes,
one star outshining

the great blazing arc
Viking longboats
steered by.

Stars bright at noon
just not given to us then.
Evening she whipstitched

edges of openwork,
hardanger holes spaced
evenly as graves,

their beauty
outlining
what's no longer there.

NOTES

Page 15: Sopa fideo—hearty soup, with vermicelli and tomato.

Pages 18 & 31: Arroyo—riverbed, usually dry.

Page 23: The barrel mentioned here is a cactus.

Page 32: Ajo lily is the flower of wild desert garlic.

Page 39: Babiche—thongs or threads made of sinew or rawhide.

Page 43: Widgeon—a 1942 amphibious airplane, which can land on its belly on water, or on its wheels on land.

Arrigetch Peaks—part of Alaska's Brooks Range, and part of The Gates of the Arctic.

Page 46: The Monsoon is a restaurant.

Page 50: "the lamp in the spine" —Virginia Woolf

Page 52: "Aubade: Morning Aurora" is for Aldona Jonaitis.

Page 78: In Northwest Coast native art, transformation masks, during dances, open to reveal several faces. They exist within one another.

Page 92: Hardanger—distinctive needlework, in diamond or square openwork patterns. It originated in a district of west Norway by the same name.